D1200411

Foods of Colombia

Barbara Sheen

KIDHAVEN PRESS
A part of Gale, Cengage Learning

Detroit • New York • San Francisco • New Haven, Conn • Waterville, Maine • London

LIBRARY OF CONGRESS CATALOGING-IN-PUBLICATION DATA

Sheen, Barbara.
  Foods of Colombia / by Barbara Sheen.
    p. cm. -- (A taste of culture)
  Includes bibliographical references and index.
  ISBN 978-0-7377-5948-8 (hardcover)
  1. Cooking, Colombian--Juvenile literature. 2. Food--Colombia--Juvenile literature. 3. Cookbooks--Juvenile literature. 4. Colombia--Social life and customs. I. Title.
  TX716.C7S54 2012
  641.59861--dc23

                                                        2011042875

Kidhaven Press
27500 Drake Rd.
Farmington Hills MI 48331

ISBN-13: 978-0-7377-5948-8
ISBN-10: 0-7377-5948-8

Printed in the United States of America
1 2 3 4 5 6 7 16 15 14 13 12

Contents

Land of Plenty

Colombia is the northernmost country in South America and the fourth largest on that continent. It is a land of contrasts. Within its borders are towering snowcapped mountains, active and inactive volcanoes, huge rivers, arid deserts, tropical rainforests, sandy beaches bordering the Pacific Ocean and the Caribbean Sea, rich farmlands, and lush grasslands. Anything and everything can thrive in Colombia's many climate zones and rich soil. As a result, Colombians have a wide variety of food choices. "Our crops are immense in variety, our animals diverse in type, shape and size. Tropical vegetation covers more than half our territory. … Mango, guava, papaya, palm and

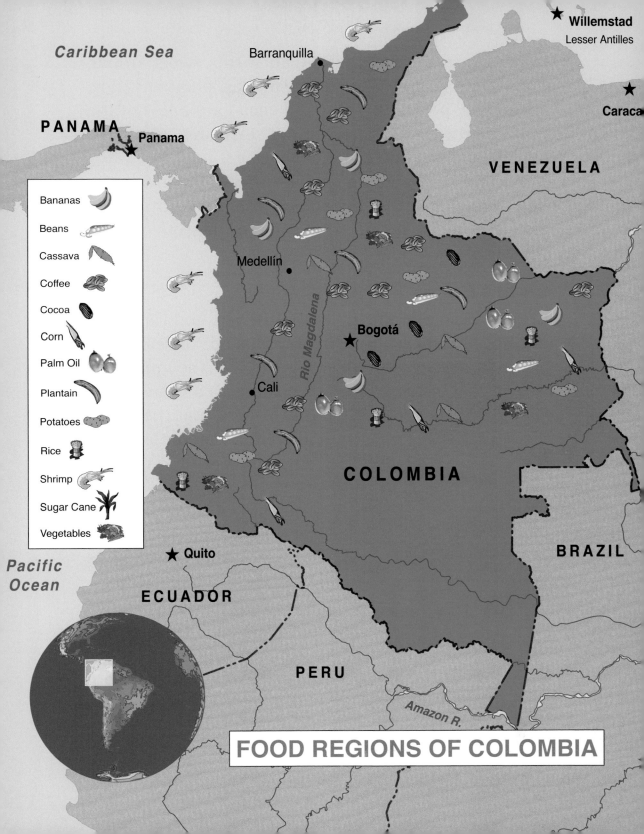

FOOD REGIONS OF COLOMBIA

many other fruit trees fill the air with a sweet aroma. Plantations of coffee bushes, bananas, plantains, rice, sugarcane, potatoes, corn, and cacao are a few of the hundreds of plants that we grow,"[1] explains Colombian author Patricia McCausland-Gallo.

Colombians take advantage of this great bounty. Yet, there are certain ingredients that they turn to day after day. These include corn, starchy vegetables, rice, fresh fruit, and meat.

Sweet Corn

Corn grows naturally in South America, and Colombians have been eating corn for thousands of years. The vegetable was so important to Colombia's native people, in fact, that they considered it sacred. Corn was not only a source of food for them, it was an important part of their religious ceremonies as well. When the Spanish first arrived in Colombia in the 16th century, they had never seen corn before. But it was not long before corn became part of their diet, too.

A vendor sells arepas con queso (with cheese) from a cart.

Interesting Facts About Colombia

- Colombia borders Panama, Venezuela, Brazil, Ecuador, Peru, the Caribbean Sea, and the Pacific Ocean.
- Colombia is about twice the size of Texas.
- Colombia's Caribbean coast is closer to Miami, Florida, than Miami is to New York.
- Colombia's capital is Bogotá. Bogotá ranks as the third major city that is highest above sea level in the world.
- Colombia is the world's second largest exporter of fresh flowers.
- Ninety percent of the world's emeralds are found in Colombia.
- African slaves were brought to Colombia to work for the Spanish from the 16th century until 1801.
- Panama was part of Colombia until 1901.
- Colombia is the oldest and most stable democracy in Latin America.
- Colombia has 85 different ethnic groups, creating a mixture of European, native, and African cultures.
- Spanish is the official language. The peso is the currency.

Modern Colombians still love corn. They eat corn on the cob dripping with butter. They add corn to stews, soups, salads, and casseroles. They also pop it and turn it into cornmeal, which they use to make **arepas** (ah-RAY-pahs).

Cheese Arepas

Arepas are made with precooked cornmeal. It is sold in North American supermarkets that carry Hispanic products under the names masarepa, masa al instante, instant masa, and harina precocida.

Ingredients
1 cup precooked cornmeal
1 cup grated mozzarella cheese
1 cup hot water
2 tablespoons butter, softened
Butter for cooking
Pinch of salt

Instructions
1. Mix together all the ingredients. Cover the mixture; let it stand for about ten minutes and until a soft dough forms.
2. Knead the dough for about a minute. Form the dough into 10–12 balls. Place the balls between plastic wrap and flatten them with a pan to about ¼-inch thick and 3–4 inches wide.
3. Melt ½ teaspoon of butter in a pan over medium heat. Fry the arepas in batches for about two minutes per side, using fresh butter for each batch. The arepas are done when they are dry and golden on the outside, and soft within.
Makes 10–12 arepas. Serves 4–5.

Arepas are cornmeal patties that Colombians eat like bread, either as a snack or as a light meal. "The arepa," explains Colombian blogger Diana Holguin, "is … a staple in most if not all Colombian kitchens and it is one of those [common] . . . foods that Colombians crave and search out whether they are at home, on the street or in another country altogether."[2]

Colombians make about 70 different kinds of arepas. They may be plain or they may be stuffed with a wide range of fillings. Chicken and avocado, fried fish, shredded pork, cheese, egg, or black beans are just a few of the many fillings. They may be baked in a brick oven, fried in oil, cooked on a griddle, or wrapped in banana leaves and cooked over an open fire.

Their appearance depends on the cook. Typically, arepas are white or yellow, depending on the type of corn they contain. They all are shaped like an English muffin. They are eaten hot and topped with butter, white cheese, condensed milk, or numerous sauces. No matter the type of corn used or the toppings, arepas have a moist, earthy flavor that Colombians find difficult to turn down.

Starchy Vegetables and Rice

Yuca (YOO-cah) is a starchy root vegetable native to Colombia's Amazon rainforest. It was also an important part of Colombia's native people's diet and remains very popular today. Also known as cassava or manioc, yuca looks like a large sweet potato. It is long and thin and covered by a tough brown skin. Inside, it contains snow-white flesh that tastes sweet and nutty when it is cooked. Colombians boil yuca and serve it as a side dish. They grind it into flour, which they use to make pan de yuca (pahn day YOO-cah). These are small rolls filled with cheese. Colombian cooks also add yuca to

The yuca root is used in many Colombian dishes.

soups and stews, where, according to *Saveur Magazine*'s deputy editor Beth Kracklauer, "The tuber [root] has a wonderful capacity [ability] to release its starch ... adding body and a velvety consistency."[3]

Potatoes are another starchy favorite. Potatoes are native to Colombia's Andes Mountains, and have long been a staple of Colombia's native people's diet. Worldwide, there are about 5,000 varieties of potatoes and about 3,000 of these grow in Colombia. Each type looks and tastes different. They can be large or small, have white, yellow, orange, or purple flesh, and taste sweet, bitter, creamy, or starchy. Colombians fry, boil, and bake potatoes. They stuff them with ground beef and eat them for breakfast or snacks. They put them in stews. And, they serve them as a hearty side dish.

Rice is another popular side dish. It was brought to Colombia by the Spanish. It grew well in northern and eastern Colombia. Today, Colombia is the second-larg-

The Columbian Exchange

The Columbian exchange is the term given to the exchange of plants, animals, culture, and diseases between Europe and the Americas following Christopher Columbus's voyage in 1492.

The Europeans who came to Colombia were from Spain. The Spaniards introduced cattle, sheep, pigs, chicken, rice, wheat, coffee, olives, sugarcane, grapes, and coffee, among other food stuffs. They also introduced horses, guns, and a new religion called Christianity. Unfortunately, they also brought with them contagious diseases that were unknown to Native Americans. These diseases killed many.

In exchange, the Spaniards took home food from the Americas unknown in their country, including corn, tomatoes, potatoes, and exotic fruits and vegetables, such as pineapple, pumpkins, yuca, squash, strawberries, various nuts, and cocoa beans.

The Columbian exchange altered life throughout the world. The Europeans introduced foods from the Americas to Asia and Africa, too. Foods like corn, peanuts, and yuca were planted in Asia and Africa and became important foods there.

est producer of rice in South America. Colombians eat about 99 pounds (45kg) of rice per person each year. In comparison, each North American eats about 21 pounds (9.5kg) per year.

In Colombia most meals include two starches. A bowl of fluffy white rice is usually one of the two. Indeed, Erica, a Colombian cook and blogger, recalls: "In my family we would eat white rice as a side dish with everything.... My grandmother ... used to get up every morning and make coffee and white rice and keep it in the rice maker warm for the day."[4] Rice is also combined with beans, chicken, or seafood and served as a main dish. It is sweetened and made into creamy desserts, too.

Wonderful Fruit

Fruit is another ingredient that shows up at many Colombian meals. Colombians eat it for dessert and snacks. They also use it to make preserves, juices, and smoothies, and they put it to use in salads. A mind-boggling variety of fruit in almost every size, shape, and color grows in Colombia. Some are familiar to most North Americans, including bananas, strawberries, blackberries, limes, oranges, and

Papayas grow abundantly in Colombia.

pineapple. Other popular fruits are less common in North American and European cultures. **Plantains**, for example, look like long green bananas. They are too hard and bitter to be eaten raw, but when fried, mashed, or boiled they taste like potatoes.

Colombian papayas are as big as watermelons. Their sweet orange flesh is a popular ingredient in smoothies. There are also five kinds of mangoes. Sweet star-shaped carambolas (cah-rahm-BOH-las) and sour lulo

Fruit Smoothie

Smoothies made with tropical fruit and milk are popular in Colombia. Banana, papaya, and mango smoothies are all delicious. This recipe uses papaya. To turn this recipe into a juice, substitute water for the milk.

Ingredients
2 cups papaya, peeled, seeded, and sliced
1½ cups milk (whole, low-fat, or soy)
1 tablespoon honey
4 ice cubes

Instructions
1. Put all the ingredients in a blender.
2. Blend on high until the mixture is smooth and frothy.
3. Pour into glasses and enjoy!
Serves 2.

Smoothies made from the papaya fruit are a common treat in Colombia.

(LOO-loh) are just a couple. As Travel Channel host Anthony Bourdain explains: "[Colombia has] . . . an extravaganza, a cornucopia [abundance] of fruits, most of which I've never heard of."[5]

A Country of Meat Lovers

Meat is another favorite ingredient in Colombian cooking. Colombians eat it for breakfast, lunch, dinner, and snacks. Colombia's rich **llanos** (YAH-nohs), or grasslands, are a perfect place to raise cattle and sheep. Located east of the Andes Mountains in Colombia and Venezuela, the llanos take up an area twice the size of the state of Nevada. Pigs and chickens, too, are raised on Colombian farms. The Spanish introduced these animals to Colombia.

Colombians roast, grill, bake, boil, and fry meat. They add it to stews and soups, fill savory pies with it, shred it and top it with tomato sauce, and boil it and grind it into a powder. No parts of the animals are wasted. For instance, Colombians deep-fry pork fat and skin to make a popular snack called **chicharrones** (chee-cha-ROH-nays). They use less tender cuts of meat to make sausages, or chorizo (choh-REE-so). And, they eat grilled or fried organ meats with gusto. As McCausland-Gallo explains: "We eat the organs, heart, liver, kidney, brain, tongue, tail, and tripe [intestines] as well as the rest of the beef. ... Children are given beef organs for their high iron contents. ... If people can afford it, meat is eaten more than five times a week. We are a meat-loving population."[6]

A basket of chicharrones makes a popular Colombian snack.

With its vast llanos, Colombia produces a large amount of meat. A wealth of other foods come from the nation's rich soil, coastal and inland waters, and varied climate zones. Colombian cooks use this wide variety of fresh ingredients creatively in many traditional recipes.

chapter

2

Recipes Have Regional Twists

Colombians insist on using fresh ingredients in their cooking. Cooks in different regions of the country often add or substitute local ingredients for those from other regions. For example, cooks in the Andes Mountains add potatoes to a recipe or use them instead of yuca or plantains. Cooks on the coast might add coconut. As a result, favorite national dishes do not always contain the same ingredients throughout the country. Despite regional differences, Colombians' favorite meals have much in common: They are made with the freshest local ingredients, are colorful, and are loaded with flavor.

A Huge Platter

Bandeja paisa (bahn-DAY-hah pah-EE-sah) is Colombia's national dish. Colombia is divided into thirty-two departments, which are similar to states. Bandeja paisa has its roots in the department of Antioquia (Ahn-tee-OH-kee-ah). It is a mountainous region located in northwestern Colombia. The people living there are known as paisas (pah-EE-sahs), or country folk. Bandeja paisa originated as a hearty lunch for farmers who spent the morning working on the coffee plantations of Antioquia. The dish contains about 1,500 **calories**, which is a lot. Most adults only need between 1,600 and 3,000 calories each day. The number of calories needed depends on a person's activity level. The more active a person is, the more calories he or she needs. For farmers doing hard physical labor from dawn until dusk, bandeja paisa provides just the energy they need.

Bandeja paisa is served on a large platter or tray, called a bandeja in Spanish. Although the exact ingredients vary depending on the cook and the district in which he or she lives, bandeja paisa always contains lots of meat and starch. A typical platter is piled high with beef, rice, red beans, chorizo, an arepa, a fried egg, bacon, chicharrones, an avocado, and fried plantains. The beef may be whole or shredded steak, ground beef, or carne en polvo (CAR-nay en POHL-voh), which is beef boiled then finely ground into a powder. Some versions include morcilla (mor-SEE-ya), or blood sausage. It is a dark-colored, earthy-tasting sausage filled with rice and bits of beef cooked in cow's blood.

Bandeja paisa, Colombia's national dish, is extremely hearty and full of calories.

Cooks in the Andes Mountains add potatoes to the platter, while those in the Amazon rainforest add fried yuca. It is topped with **aji** (AH-hee), a thick, mildly spicy sauce made with tomatoes, onions, sweet and hot peppers, vinegar, and lime juice. Colombians use aji in much the same way North Americans use ketchup.

The dish is loved by Colombians. As food blogger Erica explains: "Bandeja paisa is probably the most

Beans Colombian Style

Red beans are a popular side dish in Colombia. They are also eaten for breakfast, and are an important ingredient in bandeja paisa.

Ingredients
1 can (15 ounces) red beans
2 tablespoons olive oil
4 garlic cloves, peeled and chopped
2 tablespoons chopped onion
1 small tomato, chopped
1 tablespoon chopped cilantro
¼ of a bell pepper, chopped

Instructions
1. Heat the oil over medium-low heat. Add the garlic, pepper, tomato, onions, and cilantro. Cook until the onions are translucent, and the pepper is soft.
2. Add the beans. Stir. Cover the pot. Cook until the mixture boils.

Serves 2–4.

popular Colombian dish. … Bandeja paisa is something I've eaten all my life and if I have to choose my last meal on earth, this is the one."[7]

Delicious Stew

Sancocho (sahn-COH-choh) is another beloved dish. *Sancocho* is a Spanish word meaning to boil slowly over low heat. And that is how this delicious stew is made. It originated in the department of Cauca (CAH-oo-cah), which is located on Colombia's Pacific Coast. But it has its roots in the cocidos (co-SEE-dohs), or meat stews, that the Spanish brought to Colombia. There are lots of different varieties of sancocho. Depending on where it is prepared and the fresh ingredients on hand, sancocho can contain either beef, pork, chicken, or fish, plus fresh corn on the cob, and various root vegetables like potatoes, yam, yuca, and carrots. "In Santander [a northwestern district] several kinds of meat are used—chicken, chorizo, beef, and pork ribs—and … root vegetables, plus cabbage, plantains, and chickpeas. … Sometimes rice is added. Sancocho from the Atlantic coast uses dried meat, which imparts [gives off] a special flavor. …This region also has sancocho de pescado, which is a simple sancocho made with coconut milk, fish, yuca, and plantains,"[8] explains author Maria Baez Kijac.

Sancocho is left on the stove to gently **simmer** for hours. This gives plenty of time for the flavors to mix together, the liquid to thicken, and the meat to become meltingly tender. It is usually prepared in a large pot.

Sancocho is a meal usually served for large groups of people, or at festive occasions.

Often, it is cooked outdoors over an open fire. This cooking method gives the stew a smoky taste and aroma. Sancocho is usually served with rice, avocado, a spritz of lime, and aji. It is colorful, slightly sweet, and brimming with flavor. It is a favorite meal for parties and large family gatherings. "Every great cooking culture has something like this," explains chef and TV host Anthony Bourdain, "something that's cooked really slowly, something where family and friends get together. ...The feel is familiar in a good way... the flavor mmm."[9]

Three Kinds of Potatoes

Soup is another delicious Colombian favorite. Colombians like to start a meal with a bowl of soup. When the soup is thick and hearty, it is a meal in itself. Ajiaco

Reheated Breakfast

Calentado (cahl-en-TAH-doh), which means "reheated" in English, is a traditional Colombian breakfast. It is made from leftovers. To make it, leftover rice, beans, and meat such as steak, ground beef, or sausage are put in a frying pan with oil, onions, tomatoes, and garlic and heated together. The hearty mixture is topped with a fried egg and served as one dish. It is served with an arepa and hot chocolate or coffee. Fried plantains or leftover potatoes are often served as a side dish.

Calentado is a very large meal. Most Colombians do not have time to eat it every day, but many people enjoy it on the weekends. It is served to guests in Colombian hotels and restaurants.

Eggs and cheese arepas are commonly part of a calentado, or Colombian reheated breakfast.

Ajiaco is a chicken and potato soup. The herb guasca gives the soup its unique flavor.

(ah-hee-AH-co) is especially popular. It comes from Colombia's capital city, Bogotá (boh-go-TAH), which is located in the Andes Mountains. The soup is made with chicken and white, purple, and golden potatoes. The white and purple potatoes retain their shape and color as they cook. The golden potatoes are known as papas criollas (PAH-pahs cree-OH-yahs). They break down during cooking and add sunny color, a buttery flavor, and creamy texture to the soup. **Guasca** (goo-AHS-cah) is an herb that grows in the Andes. It gives the soup its special flavor. It has a unique, somewhat bitter taste. Colombians say there is no substitute for guasca. Without it the soup would not be ajiaco.

Ajiaco usually contains carrots, onions, and garlic, too. It is served with plates of corn on the cob, sliced avocado, heavy cream, aji, and capers. Capers are pickled flower buds that come from a plant that was brought to Colombia by the Spanish. Diners add what-ever they like to their soup.

The soup is served in Colombian homes year round. "For me this is the ultimate comfort [homey] food, and it's also my favorite food from my years overseas,"[10] says Andrea Meyers, a blogger who lived in Colombia.

Made with Rice

Dishes that feature rice are other favorites. Rice and beans, chicken and rice, and coconut rice are popular choices. Rice mixed with red beans is a common Colombian meal. Arroz con pollo (ah-ROHS con POH-yo), or chicken with rice, is a colorful family staple. Most

Coconut Rice

Canned coconut milk is sold in most supermarkets. Coconut rice tastes good served with fish and fresh fruit.

Ingredients
2 cups long-grain white rice
4 cups coconut milk
½ teaspoon salt
1 tablespoon sugar

Instructions
1. Put all the ingredients in a pot. Bring to a boil over medium heat.
2. Reduce the heat to low. Cover the pot. Cook for about 20 minutes or until the liquid is evaporated and the rice is soft and fluffy.

Serves 4.

Coconut rice can be garnished with fresh coriander.

Colombians eat it at least once a week. To make it, Colombians cook chicken, rice, onions, tomatoes, bell peppers, green peas, and garlic broth until all the liquid is absorbed and the chicken is soft and tender; the rice is moist and fluffy, and the vegetables are sweet and juicy.

Coconut rice is another top choice. It is prepared by cooking rice in coconut milk. The coconut milk is a liquid made from grated coconut meat mixed with coconut juice, the clear liquid found inside a coconut. Cooking rice in coconut milk gives it a rich creamy taste and an exotic scent. Some cooks toss bits of fried coconut in the rice, which gives the dish color and crunch. The rice is served topped with a whole fried fish. On the coasts, the fish used is a saltwater fish like red snapper that may have been pulled from the ocean only moments before it was cooked. This meal is served at one of many casual eateries that dot Colombia's beaches. Patricia McCausland-Gallo recalls: "I would have it [fried fish and coconut rice] every Sunday at the beach when I was a teenager. They sold the fish with … coconut rice from small wooden houses right on the beach."[11] Inland, the fish is a freshwater fish, like trout or tilapia. Whether freshwater or saltwater fish, the meal is delicious—moist, tender, and aromatic.

Indeed, no matter the recipe, Colombia's favorite dishes are packed with flavor. Fresh local ingredients help make them so.

3

A Snack Before Supper

Most Colombians do not eat supper until 8 or 9 P.M. To keep from getting too hungry during the day, Colombians often have a late-afternoon snack. Street vendors, little cafés, restaurants, bakeries, juice stands, and food stalls can be found everywhere. They fill the air with enticing aromas. Vendors tempt passers-by with all kinds of hot and cold, sweet and savory, and liquid and solid treats.

Colombian Coffee

Many Colombians take an afternoon coffee break, but anytime is considered a good time to drink coffee in Colombia. Colombians sip the hot beverage day and night.

A Colombian coffee farmer harvests beans.

Coffee was first grown in Africa. It was brought to Colombia by Spanish priests in the 18th century. Today coffee is Colombia's largest crop and biggest export. Many people consider Colombian coffee to be the best in the world. Coffee is so important to Colombia's economy that before being allowed to cross the border, all cars entering the nation are sprayed in order to kill any bacteria that could harm coffee plants.

Harvesting coffee is not simple. Coffee comes from beans found within the fruit of coffee trees. The trees thrive in the foothills of the Andes Mountains. The fruit looks like hard cherries and Colombians pick it by hand. Then they spread the fruit out in the air to dry for about a week. Once dried, the outer layer of the fruit is removed and the coffee bean is uncovered. The

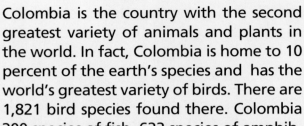

Many Species

Colombia is the country with the second greatest variety of animals and plants in the world. In fact, Colombia is home to 10 percent of the earth's species and has the world's greatest variety of birds. There are 1,821 bird species found there. Colombia is also home to 3,200 species of fish, 623 species of amphibians, 467 species of mammals, and 518 species of reptiles. Red howler monkeys, jaguars, ocelots, bats, Andean bears, condors, tree frogs, red-banded poison frogs, mountain tapirs, whistling ducks, red-tailed squirrels, giant anteaters, crocodiles, gold plumed parakeets, and dozens of different varieties of hummingbirds are just a few of these animals.

About one-sixth of the world's butterfly species also lives in Colombia. A mind-boggling 51,220 species of plants can be found there, too. There are 3,000 species of orchids alone. This is the largest collection on earth. What is even more amazing is that new animal and plant species are being discovered in Colombia all the time.

beans must be roasted before they can be used. They are placed in rotating drums, which are heated to 550°F (288°C). The heat and motion cause the beans to pop, turn brown, and release oil that gives coffee its flavor and fragrance.

Colombian coffee is especially fragrant. It has a rich, mild flavor that Colombians love. Even children drink coffee in Colombia. They add lots of milk and sugar and have it with breakfast. Adults often would rather sip strong black **tinto** (TEEN-toe), which means ink in Spanish. Tinto is similar to the strong, dark coffee drink known as espresso. Both drinks are served in tiny cups. Getting together with friends over tinto is part of Colombian daily life.

Hot Chocolate

Drinking hot chocolate with friends is another favorite activity. Chocolate is made from cacao beans. These beans grow in Colombian rainforests. The beans are picked and then turned into sweet, delicious chocolate right in Colombia. To make hot chocolate, Colombians use blocks of chocolate that are made to melt in hot liquid. The liquid can be either cow's milk, coconut milk, or water. This liquid is added to the chocolate and heated in a tall pot known as a chocolatera (choh-coh-lah-TAY-rah). Once the chocolate melts, cooks whip the mixture with a **molinillo** (mo-lee-NEE-yo). This is a special wooden whisk that cooks stick into the melted chocolate and roll the other end between their palms. The rolling whips the chocolate mixture until a foamy froth forms. Colombians say that the thicker the foam the better the hot chocolate. Blogger Andrea Meyers recalls:

> Hot chocolate … was pretty much part of daily life [in Colombia], and I loved to watch it being prepared. The locals used an aluminum pitcher called a chocolatera to warm milk or water on the stove, then they added chocolate as well as sugar if needed. After the

Cinnamon sticks, chocolate, and a molinillo are used to make Colombian hot chocolate.

chocolate was melted they would use a wooden molinillo to froth the chocolate. They'd put the round business end of the wooden stick in the bottom of the pitcher and roll the handle quickly between their hands as if they were trying to start a fire. The chocolate would froth up the sides of the pitcher, but the tall round shape that tapered near the top kept the chocolate from splattering over. Once it was well-frothed, they poured the steaming chocolate into cups. ... Colombia was where I learned how good hot chocolate could be.[12]

The delicious foamy liquid is sold in Colombian cafés, restaurants, and from street stalls. Many Colombians stop for a cup on their way home from work. It is often served with a chunk of sweet white cheese that Colombians drop into the hot chocolate. The cheese quickly melts and thickens the already rich and creamy drink. Little rolls filled with cheese and arepas spread with butter are also popular light-and-tasty accompaniments to coffee or hot chocolate.

Savory Favorites

Other favorite snacks like empanadas (em-pah-NAH-dahs) are more filling. Empanadas are delicious stuffed pastries filled with meat. They originated in Spain and are popular throughout Latin America.

Colombia has many versions of empanadas. Colombian empanadas can be round or half-moon shaped. They can be made with bread dough or crisp, chewy cornmeal dough. They can be filled with shredded beef, ground beef and potatoes, a mixture of pork and beef, or chicken. Making them is not simple. First the

A woman sells a variety of empanadas in the main town square.

Colombian Hot Dogs

Hot dogs are a popular snack in Colombia. There are hot dog stands in all of Colombia's big cities. Colombians like their hot dogs smothered with toppings. Melted white cheese and hardboiled egg are often added to the toppings in this recipe. Mashed avocado and chopped onions are also popular toppings.

Ingredients
4 hot dogs
4 hot dog buns
4 teaspoons chopped onions
4 teaspoons crushed potato chips
4 teaspoons pineapple, cut in small chunks
4 teaspoons coleslaw
2 teaspoons mayonnaise
2 teaspoons ketchup

Instructions
1. Boil water in a pot. Add the hot dogs. Cover the pot. Cook over medium heat for about 6–8 minutes and until the hot dogs are cooked throughout.
2. Remove the hot dogs from the pot. Drain them on a paper towel.
3. Mix the mayonnaise and ketchup together. Spread a teaspoon of the mixture on each bun.
4. Put a hot dog in each bun. Top with coleslaw, pineapple, onion, and potato chips.

Serves 4.

cook must make the dough and the filling separately. Once the filling is cooked, it is spread on the dough. Next, the cook folds the empanada and seals the edges by moistening them with egg. Finally, the empanadas are deep fried in sizzling-hot oil. They are ready when they are moist on the inside and golden on the outside.

The pastries are easy to handle and therefore perfect for eating on the run. They are sold by street vendors, in bakeries, and in little mini-markets that Colombians run out of their homes. Colombians eat empanadas piping hot with aji and a slice of lemon, which they squeeze over the top. They taste crunchy, juicy, meaty, and delicious. According to Jackie, a Colombian American blogger, "They are eaten throughout Colombia year round as breakfast or a snack; you can also get them at any Colombian restaurant or bakery in the U.S.… These are so good and almost addicting, you can't just have one!"[13]

Sweet Treats

Sweet treats are also popular snacks, especially if they contain arequipe (ah-ray-KEE-pay) or fruit. Arequipe is caramel cream. It is also known as manjar (mahn-HAR) in other parts of Latin America, and dulce de leche (DOOL-say day LAY-chay) in Spain, where it was invented. The cream is made by simmering milk and sugar until a thick, very sweet toffee-colored paste forms. Making it takes time and patience. Cooks must constantly stir the mixture until it thickens. This takes about an hour. Ready-made tubs of arequipe are sold everywhere, making it easy for busy Colombians to enjoy this sugary treat. Schoolchildren often carry single-serving-sized tubs in their lunchboxes.

Colombians eat arequipe by the spoonful. They

More Sweets

Colombians like sweets. Most have a sweet snack midmorning and another in the late afternoon. Sweet desserts are an important part of meals. Flan (flahn), a sugary yellow custard topped with a caramel crust is a popular dessert. So is arroz con leche (ah-ROHS cohn LAY-chay), a rich, creamy rice pudding.

Sweets featuring coconut are other favorites. Coconut pie is the most famous dessert of Cartagena (cahr-tah-GAY-nah), an old and beautiful walled city on the Caribbean Sea. Cocadas (coh-CAH-dahs), coconut candies made of shredded coconut cooked in sugar water, are a coastal specialty too. They are sold on beaches.

Dulces (DOOL-says), or preserves, are another Colombian treat. They are made by boiling chunks of fruit in sugary syrup. Popular dulces feature figs; mamey, a sweet brown fruit with orange pulp; raspberries; or papaya. Colombians eat dulces by the spoonful, like pudding or flavored gelatin.

Sweet shops are found throughout Colombia. This shop is in the old town of Cartagena, Colombia.

Salpicón

Any fruits can be used in salpicón. The juice is usually taken from fresh watermelons. However, the ingredients can be changed to suit the cook and the type of fresh fruit available.

Ingredients
3 cups of assorted fruit, cut in small chunks (bananas, strawberries, pineapple, mango, grapes)
1 cup fruit juice (watermelon, cranberry, or orange)
3 scoops vanilla ice cream
3 teaspoons shredded coconut

Instructions
1. Divide the fruit among three tall dessert glasses. Pour one-third of a cup of juice into each glass. Stir.
2. Top with one scoop of ice cream per glass and a teaspoon of shredded coconut.

Serves 3.

top ice cream with it, dip fruit into it, and spread it on obleas (oh-BLAY-ahs). Obleas are large, crisp, round wafers that taste like waffle ice cream cones.

Fruit serves as the star attraction in many Colombian snacks. Fruit smoothies, freshly made fruit juices, and fruit-flavored ice cream are favorites. So is salpicón (sahl-pee-COHN). Salpicón is a delicious fruit cocktail sold from colorful fruit carts. According to chef and blogger Diana Holguin, the carts "are everywhere, all the time, every day, selling cups of papaya, mango, green mango, assorted fruit cups with toppings like coconut, cream, condensed milk, and freshly pressed orange juice—a fruit-lovers paradise. My absolute favorite snack is the salpicón."[14]

Salpicón contains bite-size pieces of assorted fruit topped with a splash of fresh watermelon juice or sparkling soda, and a scoop of vanilla ice cream. Some cooks add an additional layer of soft white cheese and/ or shredded coconut. Although the combination of cheese and ice cream may sound odd, the mild-tasting cheese adds a pleasant saltiness to the refreshing sweet treat.

Salpicón, coffee, frothy hot chocolate, juicy empanadas, fluffy rolls, and delicate wafers topped with arequipe, are just a few of the many treats sold on Colombia's streets. There are also hamburgers and hot dogs topped with anything and everything, rich creamy ice cream, fried plantain chips, herbal teas, and fresh coconut milk, to name just a few items. With so many delicious treats available, it is no wonder that snacking is a regular part of Colombian life.

Party Time

Colombians love to get together and celebrate. Any occasion is a chance to have a party. Music, dancing, and special foods are essential parts of Colombian celebrations.

Welcoming the Christmas Season

Christmas is a festive time of the year in Colombia. According to Colombian food blogger Nika Boyes, Christmastime is "quite a production…. It can be exhausting if you are not used to partying constantly for a better part of some 15 days."[15]

The Christmas season officially begins at dusk on December 7. On that day Colombians light rows of skinny candles outside their homes and the govern-

Public areas of Colombia are brilliantly lit up for the Christmas festivities.

ment decorates public areas with thousands of glittering colored lights. Colombians hail the start of the holiday season with a party. The festivities continue on December 16. Traditionally, from December 16 to December 24, families, friends, and neighbors get together every night to pray, sing Christmas carols, and feast on traditional holiday foods. Often family members rotate hosting the celebration. Buñuelos (boon-yoo-WAY-lohs), and natilla (nah-TEE-ya) are a part of almost every holiday event.

Buñuelos are tasty fried dough balls that are popular throughout Latin America. Each country has its own version. Colombian buñuelos are savory treats made with creamy soft white cheese mixed with cornstarch to form a rich dough. The mixture is shaped into little balls and fried in hot oil. The trick is getting the oil temperature just right. If it is too hot, the buñuelos burn; if it is too cool, the dough turns out soggy. When the oil temperature is perfect, so are the buñuelos—crispy and golden on the outside, and soft and cheesy within.

Bakeries all over Colombia sell buñuelos. Even so, many Colombians like to make their own. Families often turn buñuelo making into part of the holiday fun. Natalia, a Colombian woman, explains: "Families … gather around the kitchen to celebrate Christmas. All generations take special part in mixing and cooking the traditional … buñuelos. … This delicacy is cooked and offered mostly during this time of the year and it cannot be missed on every table at the end of the meal."[16]

Usually buñuelos are accompanied by natilla, a custard-like sweet made with milk and cornstarch, flavored with cinnamon, and sweetened with **panela** (pahn-AY-

Buñuelos, fried dough balls, are a traditional Colombian holiday treat.

Baked Plantains

Fried plantains are often served as appetizers at parties. They are also a popular side dish for daily and festive meals. To make this dish healthier, this recipe bakes the plantains instead of frying them. The taste is quite similar.

Ingredients
2 ripe plantains
2 tablespoons vegetable oil
Salt to taste

Instructions
1. Preheat the oven to 450°F.
2. Cut the ends off the plantains. Peel and slice the plantain on the diagonal into ½–1 inch thick slices.
3. Spray a cookie sheet with nonstick spray.
4. Put the plantain slices on the cookie sheet. Using a food brush, brush oil on each slice. Bake the plantains until they are soft and golden brown, 10–15 minutes. Salt to taste.

Serve hot. Serves 2.

Plantain chips are a tasty snack.

lah). Panela is a dark-brown by-product of sugarcane. It is sold in blocks and tastes like brown sugar. It is popular throughout South America and Central America, where it is known by many names. Colombia is South America's largest producer of panela, and more people eat it here than anywhere else in the world.

Natilla originated in Spain, where it was made with white sugar rather than panela. It was brought to Colombia by Spanish nuns. The Colombian version of natilla is sweet, thick, and creamy. Some cooks add coconut to the custard, which gives it a tropical flavor. Usually, it is cut into little squares and eaten with buñuelos. Jairo, a Colombian man, explains: "You eat [natillas] separately. First you bite a piece of natilla and after that you bite your buñuelo. [It's] just delicious."[17]

Christmas Dinner

The festivities continue on December 24—Christmas Eve—when families and friends gather to eat Christmas dinner. Menus vary from house to house and region to region. However, tamales (tah-MAH-lays) and stuffed turkey are usually part of the meal.

Turkeys are native to the Americas. Colombia's native people were eating turkey long before the Spanish arrived. Turkey remains a local favorite, especially at Christmastime. In the past, most Colombians bought live turkeys when the Christmas season began. They fed the birds well. When it was time to kill the animals for food, the birds were made to drink aguardiente (ah-goo-ahr-dee-EN-tay). Colombians believed this strong

Carnivál

For religious reasons, many Colombians give up favorite foods in the forty-day period before Easter known as Lent. For four days before the start of Lent, people in Barranquilla (bahr-on-KEE-yah), a city on the Caribbean coast of Colombia and the birthplace of pop singer Shakira, throw a huge street party known as Carnivál (car-nee-VAHL). Barranquilla's Carnivál is the second biggest and most grand in the world. It opens with the reading of a statement saying that everyone must have fun.

During Carnivál, Colombians wear colorful costumes, dance in the streets, and hold parades with music bands and floats decorated with real and paper flowers. Dance groups performing traditional folk dances and modern Latin dances, and musical groups performing many styles of Colombian music compete against each other. As part of the fun, people throw water on each other. Food and beverages are available from street vendors.

Dancers wear traditional masks during the Colombian Carnivál celebration.

Tamales, pictured, and turkey are served at the Colombian Christmas dinner table.

alcoholic beverage made the animals' last moments happy. Many Colombians still do this, while others buy ready-to-cook turkeys in butcher shops and supermarkets.

Colombians cook turkey by roasting it in the oven. Before the turkey is roasted, it is washed with lime juice, which cleans, scents, and tenderizes the meat. Then, butter that is flavored with spices is rubbed on the bird's skin. Finally, the turkey is stuffed with a sweet, salty, spicy mixture of pork, beef, bacon, spices, bread crumbs, prunes, apples, raisins, onions, olives, and almonds. As the bird cooks, the many flavors mix

Tres Leches Cake

Tres leches (trace LAY-chays) cake means three-milk cake. It is served throughout Colombia, and is almost always a part of festive events. To make it easier to prepare, this recipe uses cake made from a cake mix.

Ingredients
1 white or yellow cake mix
1 12-ounce can evaporated milk
1 14-ounce can sweetened condensed milk
1 cup half-and-half
1 teaspoon vanilla
1 cup whipped topping
¼ cup shredded coconut

Instructions
1. Make the cake according to the directions on the package. Let it cool for 30 minutes.
2. Mix together the three milks and the vanilla.
3. When the cake is cool, using a fork or bamboo skewer poke holes in the cake about ½-inch apart.
4. Pour the milk mixture over the cake. Leave the cake out for about 15 minutes or until most of the liquid soaks in.
5. Cover the cake with foil and put it in the refrigerator overnight.
6. Before serving, mix the coconut with the whipped topping. Spread it over the top of the cake.

Serves 8.

A tres leches cake, or three milk cake, is usually incorporated into a Colombian celebration.

and mingle and fill the turkey with a delicious blend of tastes and aromas.

The turkey is done when the skin is golden and crispy, and the meat is tender and juicy. Before it is brought to the table, the rich, flavorful stuffing is removed from the turkey. It is served alongside the bird.

Tamales are served with the turkey. Tamales are steamy dough pockets filled with savory or sweet ingredients. They are wrapped in corn husks or banana leaves and tied with a string. This makes them look as though they are little Christmas packages. Tamales are one of the earliest foods of the native people of South America. They are eaten in all the countries of the continent. They have many different names and many variations. Colombia alone has dozens of regional varieties. Colombian tamales can be made of cornmeal, yuca flour, or rice. They can be filled with many different ingredients in numerous combinations. Pork, chicken, and sausage; white cheese, lemon peel, and raisins; chicken, potatoes, and chickpeas; and pork and hard-boiled eggs are just a few of the possibilities.

Whatever the variety, making tamales takes time and effort. Cooks must soak and clean the corn husks or banana leaves, mix and knead the dough, prepare and cook the filling, put the tamales together, carefully wrap them, tie them closed with a string, then stack them in a large pot and steam them until they are hot and tender. Usually family members work together in a production line to accomplish the task. "This is best done surrounded by all of your favorite relatives (preferably mamas, abuelitas [grandmothers], and tias [aunts] who know how to do this and who have all sorts of stories to tell) so that you have help and make it all go by quickly,"[18] Boyes explains.

When the little packets are served, the cooks are rewarded for their hard work. When diners unwrap the tamales, they are greeted by a burst of steam, a mouthwatering aroma, and a delicious taste that makes Christmas extra special.

Roasted Pig

Lechona (lay-CHOH-nah) is the Spanish word for roasted pig, which is another special Colombian food. Colombians hold large family gatherings for holidays, birthdays, weddings, anniversaries, or other special occasions, and lechona is often served at those events. Lechona consists of a whole pig that is split open and **deboned**, except for its legs and feet. The carcass is stuffed with rice, pork, chickpeas, potatoes, and lard, which is white, slightly soft pig fat. As the pig cooks, the lard melts and moist-

The lechona, or roasted pig, is the highlight of Colombian celebrations.

ens the other ingredients. The animal's skin is rubbed with orange juice, coconut water, and spices. The mixture keeps the skin crispy and moist as it cooks. It also gives the skin a warm golden glow and a sweet citrusy taste. Slits are cut into the animal's skin, too. The juice

Meeting Difficult Challenges

In recent years, Colombia has met some difficult challenges. One was the fight against drug trafficking. For a time, the illegal growing, processing, and selling of marijuana and cocaine was a major source of income for some Colombians. Rich and powerful illegal-drug organizations known as cartels searched for young people to be workers. Many youth were forced to join. Conflicts between different drug-trafficking groups caused violence throughout Colombia. Many innocent people were hurt or killed.

Another challenge for Colombia was keeping the people safe from the violence caused by terrorists and illegally armed groups who tried to overturn the government. These groups also kidnapped people and held them for ransom. Although these problems are not completely solved, the Colombian government has worked hard to deal with the violence. As a result, in the last few years Colombia has become a much safer place. In fact, as a nation, the entire country of Colombia now reports less crime than many American cities.

drips through the slits onto the stuffing, adding additional flavor and moistness. Before it is cooked, the pig is sewn up so that it looks whole. It is then placed on a large pointed rod called a spit. The spit is placed in a brick oven, where the pig will cook for about ten hours. Since one pig can feed 60 to 80 people, it takes a long time to cook.

When it is ready, the pig is brought to the table on a huge glistening platter, which usually takes two people to carry. To add to the drama, the pig is often surrounded by fresh fruit. But it is the taste that is most spectacular. The combination of crackling crisp skin, juicy meat, and fat-moistened rice is irresistible.

Special foods like lechona add to the excitement and fun of Colombian celebrations. Colombians love to have parties. The company of friends and family, music, dancing, and festive foods help make every get-together more memorable.

Metric Conversions

Mass (weight)

1 ounce (oz.)	= 28.0 grams (g)
8 ounces	= 227.0 grams
1 pound (lb.) or 16 ounces	= 0.45 kilograms (kg)
2.2 pounds	= 1.0 kilogram

Liquid Volume

1 teaspoon (tsp.)	= 5.0 milliliters (ml)
1 tablespoon (tbsp.)	= 15.0 milliliters
1 fluid ounce (oz.)	= 30.0 milliliters
1 cup (c.)	= 240 milliliters
1 pint (pt.)	= 480 milliliters
1 quart (qt.)	= 0.96 liters (l)
1 gallon (gal.)	= 3.84 liters

Pan Sizes

8-inch cake pan	= 20 x 4-centimeter cake pan
9-inch cake pan	= 23 x 3.5-centimeter cake pan
11 x 7-inch baking pan	= 28 x 18-centimeter baking pan
13 x 9-inch baking pan	= 32.5 x 23-centimeter baking pan
9 x 5-inch loaf pan	= 23 x 13-centimeter loaf pan
2-quart casserole	= 2-liter casserole

Temperature

212° F	= 100° C (boiling point of water)
225° F	= 110° C
250° F	= 120° C
275° F	= 135° C
300° F	= 150° C
325° F	= 160° C
350° F	= 180° C
375° F	= 190° C
400° F	= 200° C

Length

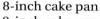

1/4 inch (in.)	= 0.6 centimeters (cm)
1/2 inch	= 1.25 centimeters
1 inch	= 2.5 centimeters

Notes

Chapter 1: Land of Plenty

1. Patricia McCausland-Gallo. *Secrets of Colombian Cooking.* New York: Hippocrene, 2004, p. 3.

2. Diana Holguin. "The Azafran Gastronomy Festival in Bogota." *Bogota Eats + Drinks*, March 18, 2010. http://bogotaeatsanddrinks .com/page/4/.

3. Beth Kracklauer. "The Cassava Variations." *Saveur*, March 2011, p. 95.

4. Erica. "White Rice (Arroz Blanco)." *My Colombian Recipes,* April 19, 2009. www.mycolombianrecipes.com/white-rice-arroz-blanco.

5. Anthony Bourdain. *No Reservations: Colombia.* The Travel Channel, 2008.

6. McCausland-Gallo. *Secrets of Colombian Cooking,* p. 51.

Chapter 2: Recipes Have Regional Twists

7. Erica. "Paisa Tray." *My Colombian Recipes*, August 4, 2009. www .mycolombianrecipes.com/paisa-tray-bandeja-paisa.

8. Maria Baez Kijac. *The South American Table.* Boston: The Harvard Common Press, 2003, p. 149.

9. Bourdain. *No Reservations: Colombia.*

10. Andrea Meyers. "Ajiaco Bogotano (Colombia)." *Andrea Meyers Making Life Delicious.* December 27, 2006, http://andreasrecipes .com/2006/12/27/ajiaco-bogotano-colombia/#more-78.

11. McCausland-Gallo. *Secrets of Colombian Cooking.* p. 102.

Chapter 3: A Snack Before Supper

12. Andrea Meyers. "Colombian Hot Chocolate." *Andrea Meyers Making Life Delicious.* December 6, 2010, http://andreasrecipes

.com/2010/12/06/colombian-hot-chocolate/.

13. Jackie. "Empanadas Colombianas (Colombian Empanadas)." *World of Jackie*, December 6, 2010. http://worldof-jackie.blogspot.com/2010/12/colombian-empanadas-emapanadas.html.

14. Diana Holguin. "Bogotá's Ciclovía Street Food." *Bogota Eats + Drinks*, March 26, 2010. http://bogotaeatsanddrinks.com/page/4/.

Chapter 4: Party Time

15. Nika Boyes. "Colombian Tamales How-2 Guide." *Nikas Culinaria*, December 29, 2006. http://nikas-culinaria.com/2006/12/29/colombian-tamales-how-2-guide/.

16. Natalia. "Christmas Traditions in Colombia." *Kiddy Travel*, December 22, 2010. www.kiddytravel.com/2010/12/christmas-traditions-in-colombia/.

17. Quoted in Nora B. "Buñuelos y Natilla—Colombian Cheese Fritters and Custard." *Life's Smorgasbord*, June 19, 2008. http://lifesmorgasbord.blogspot.com/2008/06/buuelos-y-natilla-colombian-cheese.html.

18. Boyes. "Colombian Tamales How-2 Guide."

Glossary

aji: A spicy sauce used as a condiment in Colombia.

arepas: Cornmeal patties that can be stuffed or plain.

calories: Units of energy-producing potential in food.

chicharrones: Deep-fried strips of pork skin and fat.

deboned: Having removed the bones.

guasca: An herb that grows in the Andes that is used in Colombian cooking.

llanos: Grasslands on which cattle are raised.

molinillo: A small wooden whisk used to make hot chocolate.

panela: A sweet, dark brown by-product of sugarcane.

plantains: Fruit that looks like green bananas but are cooked like a vegetable before eating; they taste like potatoes.

simmer: To cook slowly over low heat.

tinto: Strong black coffee that is served in little cups.

yuca: A starchy root vegetable also called cassava or manioc that is native to Colombia's Amazon rainforest.

for further Exploration

Books

Cheryl Blackford. *Colombia.* Minneapolis: Lerner, 2011. Readers are taken on a tour of Colombia, with the focus on the landscape, culture, people, capital, and the flag.

David Downing. *Colombia.* South Yarra, Victoria, Australia: Macmillan Education Australia, 2010. Looks at the problems and issues facing Colombia; with photos and maps.

Rebecca Thatcher Muria. *We Visit Colombia.* Hockessin, DE: Mitchell Lane, 2010. This colorful book looks at Colombia's geography, people, and culture.

Websites

Central Intelligence Agency, "World Factbook Colombia" (www.cia.gov/library/publications/the-world-factbook/geos/co.html). Information on Colombia's geography, people, government, economy, and the challenges found there.

Every Culture.com, "Colombia" (www.everyculture.com/Bo-Co/Colombia.html). Looks at Colombia's geography, history, food, economy, patriotic symbols, industries, and daily life.

How Stuff Works, "History of Colombia" (http://history.howstuffworks.com/south-american-history/history-of-colombia.htm). A summary of Colombia's history is presented here.

National Geographic Kids, "Colombia" (http://kids.nationalgeographic.com/kids/places/find/colombia/). Readers can find facts about Colombia's geography, culture, history, and wildlife; with colored photos, video, map, and an e-postcard.

Index

dulce de leche, 35, 37
dulces, 36

E
empanadas, *33,* 33–35
espresso, 31

F
fish and coconut rice, 27
flan, 36
fruit, 4, 6, 12–13, *13,* 15
  baked plantains recipe, 42, *42*
  dulces, 36
  salpicón, 37–38
  smoothies, 12, 14, *14,* 37

G
guasca, 25

H
herbs, 25
holidays
  Carnival, 44, *44*
  Christmas, 39–41, *40, 41,* 43,
    45, 45–48
hot chocolate, 31–33, *32*
hot dog recipe, 34

L
lechona, *48–49,* 48–51
llanos, 15
lulo, 13

M
mangos, 14–15
manioc, 9–10, *10*

manjar, 35, 37
masa. *See* corn
meals
  breakfast, 23, *23*
  Christmas dinner, 43, 45, *45,*
    47
  starches in, 12
  supper time, 28
meat, 15–16
  arroz con pollo, 25, 27
  bandeja paisa, 18, *19,* 20–21
  lechona, *48–49,* 48–51
  sancocho, 21–22, *22*
  turkey, 43, 45, 47
molinillos, 31, 32, *32*

N
natilla, 41, 43
national dishes
  bandeja paisa, 18, *19,* 20–21
  regional differences, 17

O
organ meats, 15

P
pan de yuca, 9
panela, 41, 43
papayas, 13, *13,* 14
pig, roasted, *48–49,* 48–51
plantains, 13, 42, *42*
plants
  coffee, 29, *29*
  Spaniards and, 11
  varieties, 4, 6, 30
  See also fruit; vegetables

Picture Credits

About the Author

Barbara Sheen is the author of more than 70 books for young people. She lived in Barranquilla, Colombia, in the 1980s. She has fond memories of the Colombian people and the delicious food, especially the tropical fruit. She now lives in New Mexico with her family. In her spare time, she likes to swim, walk, garden, and read. Of course, she loves to cook!